Blue Atlas

BOOKS BY SUSAN RICH

Poetry:

Gallery of Postcards and Maps: New and Selected Poems (2022)

Cloud Pharmacy (2014)

The Alchemist's Kitchen (2010)

Cures Include Travel (2006)

The Cartographer's Tongue (2000)

Anthologies:

Demystifying the Manuscript: Essays and Interviews on Creating a Book of Poems (2023) with Kelli Russell Agodon

The Strangest of Theaters: Poets Crossing Borders (2013) with Ilya Kaminsky and Brian Turner

Blue Atlas

poems

Susan Rich

Red Hen Press | *Pasadena, CA*

Cover photograph used with kind permission of Niranj Vaidyanathan.

Book layout by Emily K Chen

Library of Congress Cataloging-in-Publication Data

Names: Rich, Susan (Poet), author.
Title: Blue atlas: poems / Susan Rich.
Description: Pasadena, CA: Red Hen Press, 2024.
Identifiers: LCCN 2023047271 (print) | LCCN 2023047272 (ebook) | ISBN
  9781636281261 (paperback) | ISBN 9781636281278 (ebook)
Subjects: LCGFT: Poetry.
Classification: LCC PS3618.I33354 B59 2024 (print) | LCC PS3618.I33354
  (ebook) | DDC 811/.6—dc23/eng/20231010
LC record available at https://lccn.loc.gov/2023047271
LC ebook record available at https://lccn.loc.gov/2023047272

The National Endowment for the Arts, the Los Angeles County Arts Commission, the Ahmanson Foundation, the Dwight Stuart Youth Fund, the Max Factor Family Foundation, the Pasadena Tournament of Roses Foundation, the Pasadena Arts & Culture Commission and the City of Pasadena Cultural Affairs Division, the City of Los Angeles Department of Cultural Affairs, the Audrey & Sydney Irmas Charitable Foundation, the Meta & George Rosenberg Foundation, the Albert and Elaine Borchard Foundation, the Adams Family Foundation, Amazon Literary Partnership, the Sam Francis Foundation, and the Mara W. Breech Foundation partially support Red Hen Press.

First Edition
Published by Red Hen Press
www.redhen.org

Acknowledgments

Heartfelt thanks to the generous editors and staff of the journals where these poems first appeared, often in slightly different forms with slightly different names.

Journals:

Alaska Quarterly Review: "Compass," "Weeping Glass," "When Mother and Father Were"; *American Academy of Poets Poem-a-Day*: "Boketto" and "Shadowbox"; *Atlanta Review*: "Market Thief"; *Bennington Review*: "Metaphors"; *Colorado Review*: "Curriculum Vitae"; *CCR Reform Jewish Quarterly*: "Pregnant with the Dead"; *Crannóg Magazine*: "Crepe Myrtle"; *December Magazine*: "Binocular Vision," "Goldfinch"; *Ekphrastic Review*: "Your Still Life Builds a Home Inside My Head"; *Field*: "Fever"; *Flint Hills Review*: "Abeyance"; *Helen* (Canada): "Brief Catalogue of a Fading Ex"; *Gettysburg Review*: "Single, Taken, Not Interested"; *Green Mountain Review*: "Attempting Speculative Fiction"; *Inklette*: "From the Dictionary of Obscure Sorrows"; *Isele Magazine*: "The One Good Eye in the Room"; *Ithaca Lit*: "Shopping for Dresses"; *Kahini*: "Arborist / Abortionist"; *Lily Poetry Review*: "High Atlas Incantation," "Medina Morning"; *MER*: "Mother Figure, Almost"; *Minnesota Review*: "Outline for Freshmen Composition"; *Moria*: "A Blessing for What is Absent"; *New England Review*: "String Theory with Heartache"; *Notre Dame Review*: "Burn Barrel / Remaking the Shadowbox"; *Phi Kappa Phi / The Forum*: "Blue Dusk"; *Plume*: "Birthday Dinner," "The Decision," "Hello, July 5th," "Paris," "This Could Happen"; *Poetry Ireland Review*: "No One Knew"; *Qu* (Canada): "Post Abortion Questionnaire—Powered by Survey Monkey"; *Quartet Journal*: "Wedding Dress"; *Sweet: A Literary Confection*: "Not Monet's Giverny"; *Tiferet Journal*: "How did I love him?"; *Tinderbox Poetry Journal*: "Try to be Done Now with Words"; and *Western Humanities Review*: "Dear H."

Anthologies:

Best of Isele Anthology: "The One Good Eye in the Room," Iskanchi Press, 2022; *Choice Words: Writers on Abortion*: "Post Abortion Question," Haymarket Books, Boston, 2020; *Jewish Poems for the New Millennium*: "Pregnant with the Dead," Ashland Poetry, OH, 2020; *Nasty Women Poets Anthology*: "In Praise of Anger," Lost Horse Press, Sandpoint, ID, 2017; *The Path to Kindness*: "Still Life with Ladder," Storey Publishing, VT, 2022; and *Practicing Poet II*: "Boketto," Terrapin Books, West Caldwell, New Jersey, 2018.

Film:

Tova Beck-Friedman, dir. *Pregnant with the Dead*, 2020.

With Gratitude

A trillion and one acknowledgments and thanks to all the people, organizations, and angels that have come together to help me in the creation of this book. It's taken ten years of my life; I could not have done it without you. A book such as this is a collage of lived experience which can occur only in community, in connection with other open-hearted individuals.

Sincere thanks to the many organizations and foundations that have supported the creation of this work: 4 Culture, the Helene Wurlitzer Foundation, and the Highline College Professional Leave Program. A giant-sized thank you to Dr. John Mosby, who has made me feel seen in my academic work and who believes in the power of poetry to edify, empower, and offer students creative pathways to reach their highest potential.

For giving their time and expertise with laughter and kindness, I am forever thankful to Kelli Russell Agodon, Elizabeth Austen, Katherine Flenniken, and January O'Neil. For local sunsets and spontaneous adventures, warmest thank you to Kristie McLean. For transatlantic packages and global support since the beginning, lifelong thanks to Geraldine Mills.

For Tuesday Night Writers that understands that revision and good food go hand in hand, gratitude to each of you: Christine Balk, Michelle Bombardier, Suzanne Edison, Katie Ellis, Susan Landgraf, and Cindy Veach.

One thousand and one hurrahs to the Poets on the Coast; you sustain and uplift me. The literary community we have built together is the kindest and most generous I've ever known. You are all amazing!

Once again, my profound thanks to Gina Formea, for her entire wheelhouse of support.

To my dearest travel companion from Ireland to Morocco, from Italy to places not yet found on any map, profound and lasting gratitude to Angie Vorhies. So thankful to Ilya for passing you that note.

To my friends Idriss Hamiouy and Jasmine Valadani, thank you for welcoming me with warmth, love, and adventure to the Atlas Mountains of Morocco; you changed my life.

Thank you to Ruby Rich and Mary Peelen for familial love, support, and enduring friendship. To my adopted brother, Mohamud Esmail—we are in this together! To Bashar, Kat, and Leyla Balleh: you're my sweet chosen family and lifelong friends wrapped up together.

To Kate Gale, Mark E. Cull, Tobi Harper Petrie, Monica Fernandez, Rebeccah Sanhueza, and the rest of the Red Hen Press family, huge thanks for the all-important and sustaining work that you do for poetry and literature in the world.

Thank you to my homeboys past and present: Duende, Quinoa, and Mr. Watson.

Lasting gratitude and love to Youssef H. Azami.

Thank you to my ancestors, known and unknown.

Contents

Apparitions

A Second Earth Orbiting a Star

The Decision

Star Map

The Blue Atlas Cedar is native to the Atlas Mountains of Morocco where they often form whole forests. As a gymnosperm, the Blue Atlas has neither flowers nor fruits. It is the hardiest species and can reproduce spontaneously from seeds.

—europeantrees.com

Hourglass

This Could Happen

If you kept walking, you would eventually step outside of yourself.
You would leave the bones of your body,

the bloodlines to all that you loved.

You would be free of breasts, liberated
from the eyes of body admirers—

to travel this earth like a star lily or skunk flower

with the forbearance of golden bees.
If you kept walking out of the self

you could begin again as seawater, as spindrift.

Don't worry, you'd say,
you're a virgin non-body, you're a witness

to ten thousand new worlds.

No lungs, no heart, no breath—
irresistible now, what might you see?

A bird's dying shudder or

lovers knotted in a plotline of release?
You're an example now

of nothing, a fountain of nowhere—

Arborist / Abortionist

Procured by anxious relatives
who demanded

a disappearing trick—

prepaid like a surcharge
for yard work done in the off-season:

his steel tool severing

a quirk of a tree limb,
attached to the nub of a stubborn bud;

he didn't question
how I appeared,

transplanted into his waiting room—

never inquired as to the coauthor
of my infinitesimal text—

although he'd memorized its map,

extracted the troublesome little branch
that obscured the golden overlook,

and restored the river view.

Metaphors

after Sylvia Plath

Three syllables—one stressed.
Unfinished dance step—unripe mango;
an infinitesimal beansprout cut back

to a nub. I'm the interrupted battle
of bullfight and god, the abandoned ballroom,
abeyant moon. Conundrum

of choice/no choice. Watermelon
seedlet, scalpel shaving, thick mead.
Hello, turned-off oven, confused stork.

I am your desired, your dreaded *almost*—
blue atlas and weeping willow—
the past, seen ahead; the necessary tomorrow.

Post-Abortion Questionnaire—Powered by Survey Monkey

1. Do you feel reluctant to talk about the subject of abortion?

In the center of the ceiling a marigold weeps

or perhaps it's an old chandelier.

Look. Inside there is an otherworldly glow,

shards illuminated in violet-pink

and layers of peeling gold leaf.

Such minds at night unfold.

2. Do you feel guilt or sorrow when discussing your own abortion?

The cabbage is a blue rose,

an alchemical strip show. They scream

when dragged from the earth,

only to find themselves plunged into boiling water.

The narrative unscrolls from cells

of what-ifs and hourglass hopes.

3. Have you found yourself either avoiding relationships or becoming overly dependent in them since the abortion?

If I could unhinge myself from myself,

attach to bookshelves, sever

my tongue, I would watch

as it grew back, rejuvenated

and ready to speak.

4. Do you have lingering feelings of resentment toward people involved in your abortion (Perhaps the baby's father or your parents)?

One must be careful what one takes

when one turns away forever:

a Tuareg scarf, two photographs,

untamed thoughts that curse, then lift—

occasionally yes, though mostly not.

5. Do you tend to think of your life in terms of "before" and "after" the abortion?

Too scared to speak my name—

not etherized upon the table—

I wore silver stirrups, blue wraparound globe.

The young nurse and I held hands—

you're doing great, she cooed.

I remained awake, awakened.

6. Have you felt a vague sort of emptiness, a deep sense of loss, or had prolonged periods of depression?

The sky no longer speaks to me directly—

and the beautiful man?

He has dropped through the floorboards

though sometimes he answers emails:

> *Thank you, our family has survived the Paris bombings.*

> *Sincere condolences on your new president.*

7. Do you sometimes have nightmares, flashbacks, or hallucinations relating to the abortion?

Never mind, I tell myself, *it's only a nightmare.*

But then I remember I'd barely gone to bed at all.
Then thirty years had passed; now thirty-one.

8. Have you begun or increased use of drugs or alcohol since the abortion, or do you have an eating disorder?

First, the fog tastes sweet, then sour—

what is identity but forged glamour?

Strong doses of celibacy taken regularly—

9. Did your relationship to, or concept of, "God," or "Karma," or "Fate" change after your abortion?

If my own voice falters, tell them

I tried not to live inside the clock

or under the skin of pomegranates.

Does anyone escape her own story—

head-on collision, nor'easter, earthquake,

the racist seeding of our country?

10. Has your self-concept or self-esteem changed since your abortion?

Once I abandoned my car in a forest of red cedar,

let it tumble down the mountain

by itself. In the next diorama there's a friend

at the wheel and she urges, *let's go on;*

build yourself like a paint color, an infant's song.

11. Are you bothered by certain sounds like machinery that makes loud noises?

Coffee grinder, dust buster,

Singer sewing machine.

Also: truck backfire, sparkler,

the sharp scrape of chair legs—

gunfire overhead, handsaws—the evening

news—aren't you?

12. Is there anything else you would like to ask?

Why does Google Maps allow blind spots?

For example, the city of Zinder, Niger?

Is it possible for one person to photograph each galaxy—

to understand this bewilderment of light?

Glass Sponge

Goldfinch

They locked me up and then
forgot me—

here in the rope-cold dark

I stammer a calligraphy of fears;
I listen to a cinema

of laughter and then its silence.

This will be my life.

The subtitles of something—
terror, imagination, or a flare

across my throat. I am not yet

four, trapped in the attic eaves
as I decipher

my sister's half-words

calming her friend's concern.
Until as if from an afterlife—

you must never tell or—

I have no memory
of which happened next:

the long-slow descent

of the ladder stairs
toward dinner, the light milkweed

shrouded air, or the goldfinch.

Mrs. Potato Head

In the basement of dove gray cement,
of bare bulbs, we jabbed plastic spikes deep into
Idaho spuds, added all-knowing eyes and ears,

yarmulkes and long beards.
In the coldness of that house,
I built an empire of miniature soaps

from Budget Inns and Howard Johnsons
for Mrs. Potato Head to drown in—
her cups and plates hanging

coupon clean. We played and played,
not knowing the lives we invented
were old flimflam landscapes

of too much work for not enough pay.
Though sometimes we'd borrow an orange
from the fruit bowl and give it a small hat,

toothpick legs, and blue magic
marker boots. We didn't need maps
or mirrors to find a way out of the echo

chamber of childhood—just
a vegetable and a fruit repurposed
for two Jewish girls in a basement

trying with spells and with death-
defying persistence
to reshape the afternoon news.

Fever

The world closed up around her
like a tangerine and she was the pith,

pasted on sticky sheets, the hours extending

into empty corridors of miracles that would
never arrive. Medicine by her bedside,

a teacup of ice cream, and then a black and white

television rolled in for the occasion, like
a trophy she had won.

Is this what the rest of her life would be—

days conspiring against her,
orange groves just a little out of reach?

She'd lie awake until 3:00 a.m. when she would unhook

her mind from the curtains
and begin the Byzantine task of recalling everything

she knew: how to tie laces, cook scrambled eggs, compose

in blue. What was life and what would it cost her?
In the year 2000 she would be forty years old.

She would have lovers, collie dogs,

a musk-scented cottage, and her own accounts—
but she'd rather sleep with the trees!

Or maybe there'd be more—

she'd turn over and watch the snow
fling itself off the roof,

eyes primed on the next future.

Pregnant with the Dead

I am a woman swollen with the history of my dead,
great-aunts and second cousins murdered

in the old country—bloated with fragments of survivors

who hid months in garbage cans, others in partisan forests;
I'm their bandaged daughters gauzed from toe to forehead

to keep safe from search patrols, from their first rapes.

Yes, I am a body awash in stories of noodle kugel, borscht—
watch the heavy arms of the women waving like sails

as they knead challah each Friday morning,

can't conceive of an afternoon free.
What can I do with the women who occupy my vertebrae,

take over my hips and tongue?

They say *coconut bars, mandel bread, hamantaschen.*
They say *that's your problem,* as they stride

into my kitchen, toss out the non-fat yogurt, the tofu treats.

It is a rumba of before and after.
And of course, many *volk* murdered—

abducted our girls, butchered our sons.

And now, my dead tell me, it's time to enjoy
a brioche—a week in *the Disneyland.*

Don't my dead deserve to mist their skin with *Shalimar*

at the airport perfume cathedrals?
Enough time spent on nightmares!

Instead, let us hike up the heat, make selfies.

And later, when it quiets on the hotel balcony,
we vanish like light vessels almost escaped out to sea.

The Day After the Abortion

If there were a psychic map of that weekend,
she would place a pushpin by the wedding dress boutique,

although she had stayed in the car,
sunk deep into the back seat, her head held low

against the door lever, scented with cat fur and coffee.
Inside the Brooklyn shop, her sister

pirouetted while her mother clapped on cue
(she watched through the window

in her mind). And simultaneously looked back
at the slide carousel of her recent breakdowns

as if at a reliquary of aerogrammes
and one West African telephone. Her engagement

abolished before she flew home, as the ex-fiancé waved
ecstatically as the airplane lifted off, as the American

doctor greeted her plainly with, *how many weeks?*
Curled deep inside her post-op body, she cursed

car seats moist with crumbs, cursed transatlantic longing,
cursed a sibling who last week cried, *I'm engaged!*

as if to marry a man were as easy as bread and jam.
In the Sahel she had wandered millet fields, entered

encampments where women held her in Tuareg robes,
stained her hands in indigo. She oriented her limbs

by sand dunes; then, directions to the next well—
immersed herself in a galaxy of bodies and erased the world

where an unborn could be vacuumed up into small pieces
so that a bride and a mother could sleep.

Try to Be Done Now with Words

Away with the language of weeping,
the angel of perfection can go hang herself

and burn her lilies of ambition, too.

Try to be done with the golden bees,
the envy of another's sainted breathing.

Instead, embrace the outer orchard—
the well-water—

our terrestrial music of shave and shower, honey and tea.

Away from the temple, forget supplicants.
Sign on for this season's *must have* boots.

What you want is what you have always wanted—

a blue fountain, Moroccan, in the Arabic
abjad, *drink and belief.* Double note of window

and world. Go past the tendrils of line-breaks to

forget dactyls and old apples—
the symbolic yew. No more words!

Tomorrow you will revel in the call of olive groves.

O brave mouth—and touch and scent—
send coherent messages through this body

like flares off a meteor shower.

You can become your own glass sponge—
move through this world—silent, astonished, undone.

Outline for Freshman Composition

Question at issue: Did you agree to an abortion to appease a sister?

Question at issue: What did you fear?

Question at issue: Are a bomb and an abortion detonated the same?

Possible thesis statement: *Maybe not* a sensible idea to allow someone else
to determine the future.

Refined Thesis Statement: *Maybe not* because appeasement, some historians
say, (see endnotes) started World War II.

Possible Topic Sentence: To acquiesce to a midterm abortion or a war
becomes expansively problematic.

Possible evidence: Irrational to follow the middle sister
who never wanted you near;

Possible evidence: she who sequestered you in the attic, made you

swear on your life she would
do it again if you told anyone.

She knew she was safe:
you—still four days away from four years old.

Afterward, you learned silence. The tilt of gravity.
The blankness, black ice on the edge of your sky.

Possible evidence:	Because for example, three decades on the abortion stays suspended in resin like a tiny scorpion, transforming anger into amber.
	Because for my body, this was motherhood's last stand.
Counter argument:	But that April you were an adult; twenty-something.
Counter argument:	Did she hold a knife to your vagina, conduct the surgery herself?
Refuting argument:	She chauffeured me there, commented on my blistered toes.
Counter argument:	But you walked into the abortionist's office, undressed, welcomed the mask of anesthesia.
Refuting Argument:	Yes. The abortionist was handsome. Bronzed in an orange kind of way.
	He flirted with my sister, laughed well, spoke of island travel.
	And then as if at the moving pictures, I disappeared
	into the gallery seats. Watched another show.

My sister gave him her number—
she'd make the appointment, the follow-up.

Refuting Argument: Wanted out. Wanted   none of it. None
                            of this   ever   happened.

[   ]   To wake and have no memory—

[   ]   Locked away without a way.

[   ]   If I didn't make the choice but it was the right choice.
                            If I made the choice but it was the wrong choice.
                            If I could go back and find my own way.

Unintended Consequences: The rest of my life.

                            I will never visit Paris
                            or acquiesce again.

                            For three decades, no words came between us.

Possible Conclusion: Yes. No. Yes. No.
                            The abortion wars come, but do not go.

Possible Conclusion: Mybodymmybodybodymyboymybodymy
                            bodymybomb—

Compass of Desire

Anatomy of Desire at the *Cactus Cafe*

Even if you misquote me about that afternoon,
pretend that desire crawled potato bug slow

between our stairway of word and feeling,
I'd still tip my mojito to the muse of hands

almost meeting, shoulders nearly touching—
the desire for human pretzels rising above

our heads in little thought balloons—
while particles of rose salt sailed toward my feet

or was that you trying to catch my attention?
We were weed-wild and wonderous—

a page torn from a blue pocket notebook
or the first hum of a feral embrace—

so much distance still to go until
the narrative writes itself, takes us home.

No One Knew

He appled and oranged me afternoons
in his bedroom. I remember there was laughter

like the sounds of dice shaken during a game
of Parcheesi. Then the tap-tap of shifting pieces

crisscrossing the board: belt buckles and braces.
We were vulcanologists experimenting

with our newly born volcanoes. Not sex—
not exactly. Just some initial reconnaissance.

I adored him/didn't adore him, by sixteen,
which fantasies had we ingested whole?

I believed in James Dean and Anna Karenina,
Smokey Robinson and The Supremes.

Back then, M. apprenticed as a projectionist
of moving images. After school, in the dark

he introduced me to *Harold and Maude.*
Matched reel-to-reel tapes

between kisses, *So I'll always know where
to find it,* Maude says as she tosses Harold's gift,

a golden ring, into the sea. And seamlessly, the film
keeps running without pause. We were each

other's first what? Our idea of what might be?
I asked everyone then for a definition

of love, or perhaps romance. Soon
the adults became embarrassed. No one knew.

Self Portrait with Market Man

The sky stayed too far away to see, everything I knew
stolen in a land without sea. The town ran

on motorcycle exhaust and goats;
men wrapped themselves in dark cloth. I knew nothing

mattered here but human gestures—hand to heart,
eyes averted, half bows.

At the market women called out, their bodies
odd-shaped lemons next to pyramids of ill-gotten jeans.

Each voice demanding, *Madame!*—and in their torn shawls—
small onions and green mangoes. What did I know?

I knew the thrust of his chest,
the carelessness—it seemed—as he faced me—

as my eye caught his by the cuts of meat—
cues I did not understand.

Until a fury fell upon his millet-tall body
pushing hard against mine as his fingers rescued

my wallet from its half-moon pocket—
not unlike the way you,

dear unfaithful lover, would later lift the blue
scarf from my almost gorgeous life.

Zinder, Niger

Birthday Dinner in the Sahara

You carried a secondhand tablecloth
like a sash across one shoulder—

your only domestic act.

And spread the torn lace
lopsidedly over ginormous desert stone.

I don't remember any bread or chocolate, or cheese—

no actual sustenance at all.
More like a ghost meal

readied for the afterlife

on a patched-together film set—
the director

famously difficult to please—

even then I played an extra
in an unfinished tableau—

which was my life.

And for some reason still craved it,
still believed—in the action, the cuts.

How did I love him—

the first sighting, without language or need—

at second sight—
as if he had already torn a piece,

exhumed the pink inside of me.

In a millet field—

without knowledge—

I conjured him from dust and air:

orphaned gecko, violet flame—

from our first nakedness in the desert,

to our nonstop ribbon of talk

like a three-dimensional arc

of tragedy, a lightning rod, a quasar of hunger?

Why did I love him/

across the equator / on a freight train / in a failing jeep—

once upon a time in a Mopti whorehouse

as the bartender prayed

while conducting low-paid women up the watchful limbs

of the baobab tree.

Who was it that loved him/

to obsession like a pop song / a West African highlife beat.

Next time / there will be no next time/

I would barricade the continent—

double-lock the windows and floors

to all that breathed in me—

plug my ears to his baritone psalms, his siren pleas.

High Atlas Incantation

Maybe we consume too much land, too much sky,
scarf plates of Majorelle blue;

gorge ourselves on the cinnamon-creviced rock
until tagine-colored mountains give way

to olive groves, to riverbeds of sand and brine,
to lemon-colored shoes on the boys we pass

as we feed off the *mellahs*, the abandoned villages,
revealing a mirage of salt road caravans.

We dine at the overlook; have a dessert of nimbus cloud
and Moroccan light as it nudges second helpings

into our bodies, slips argon trees under our tongues.
What can we do except stand and stretch—

make room for another casbah
with silk-brocaded walls, with to-die-for

cedar doors, and an upside-down boat—
inexplicably dangling from the ceiling?

And whether we notice it, we inhale the bone marrow soup
rising from ten thousand corpses

once starved beneath these marble floors;
we gaze over human skeletons with severed heads

at the end of a pink-frosted road. And everywhere—
men hawking baskets of fossils, men selling red stone.

Wedding Dress

which was designed by the neighborhood tailor,
Alhaji, who became friend, became lover
of my black coffee and fragmented conversation

in French; of the width, the cut, the strength
of the wraparound sash of The Most
Rapturous fit—soft tint of a Saharan sky—

of the dress I modelled against
a sandstone wall. Against the past, against the body
we live in now, there lives this promise:

the West African wedding wrap
sequestered in the back of the closet.
The cloth now spiritual, sized extra small,

with seams hand-sewn by elongated fingers.
Who was the girl locked inside the alchemical stitch—
soon to create such a symphonic mess of it—

Apparitions

Boketto

Outside my window it's never the same—
some mornings jasmine slaps the house, some mornings sorrow.

There is a word I overheard today, meaning lost,
not on a career path or across a floating bridge:

Boketto—to stare out windows without purpose.
Don't laugh; it's been too long since I leaned

into the morning: bird-friendly coffee and blueberry toast.
Awhile since I declared myself a prophet of lost cats—blind lover

of animal fur and feral appetites. Someone should #hashtag
a word for the ashes of an almost marriage. Knowledge

that the heat might not hold or our lights remain on—a second
sight that drives the particulars of a life: sea glass and salt,

cherry blossoms and persistent weeds. What assembles in the middle
distance beyond the mail truck; have I overlooked oceans,

ignored crows? I try to exist in the somehow, the might still be
gaze upward to constellations of in-between.

Once Mother and Father Were Buried

After the garlic press, the musical penny bank,
the silverware from a rosewood box
were presented, argued over, stripped bare—

after the claiming of the Seder plate, inlaid
Aladdin table, and father's Hamilton watch—
after the aftermath of familial negotiations,

what did we learn of belongings?
Blue-inked scraps of paper, objects
conjured 1, 2, 3, from the lawyer's yellow pad—

the social worker's fee. War raged on in the land
of damaged goods, the cellar of used light bulbs.
Stubborn and angry as the ancestors before us,

we raised red flags—armed for total sibling divorce.
Stoic in our straight-backed chairs, our spines
taut as if sparring with an earthquake—

then our lives cracked open.

Years After, Continually Nightmared

If you would leave me in peace—but instead you accompany me to parties,
ski weekends, blues cafes. You float by at a distance—slight glimmer

from the far corner of the bar and look—sexy as ever—mean as a brilliant accountant
is mean, without malice. You stare at my body, track its pounds per inch

through the world. Observe the scarf, the lipstick. You come from behind,
saunter nearer, note my salary, my car payment—divide and itemize the economics

of our three-country breakup, our *so long*. You jot it down in inscrutable lines
and then as if in a film noir, you disappear into smoke, into jazz riffs—

defined again by your decision, as I am: cleaving closer to this spectral goodbye.

The Abortion Question

The abortion question is did you want it?
The abortion question is did you have a choice?

The abortion happened in Manhattan—

the Big Apple shaken and stirred along Madison Avenue—
just two days after being kicked out of his 5th floor Paris walk-up.

The abortion question watches you through sideview mirrors—

the self-satisfied gaze like that of an undertaker,
as if it holds the answer

to the future of your body.

∼

The abortion question loves to flirt. It flirts

with your sister who accompanies you.
Flirt rhymes with skirt and you relinquish yours

for a paper gown. The abortion question laughs

with your sister (executor of the plan) who
giggles back. But where is the deadbeat non-dad?

Is he hiding in the hourglass, the dying tulips?

∼

Such a checked-out father-not-to-be.
The abortion question is bone-tired; multilingual and global;

it looks back on its past, its coat hangers

and back alleys, the wild herbs—
cotton rootbark and black cohosh.

Take ¼ cup pennyroyal water, 12 drops hartshorn,

wrote Ben Franklin in his popular recipe
for fixing "the misfortune."

⁓

The abortion question likes the founding mothers best—
the midwives, crones, nurses,

who created an underground network:

a Jane Collective for the women
who—

fell into trouble, turned suicidal.

⁓

Abortion is no joke to this body which ate
enough for two: kosher pickle and chip sandwiches

well into the second trimester.

The abortion question places its miniature sticks
into the cervix—

small bundles of twigs made from seaweed.

See you tomorrow! The abortion question waves.
And tomorrow and tomorrow and tomorrow and tomorrow and tomorrow

⁓

This is not an anti-abortion poem.
No one will be killed with a 22-caliber rifle

as in the two women's health clinics in my hometown.

No one pushing fetus porn outside the central post office.
But the abortion question really loves to attract attention.

It lives in a clock tower, chimes strongest at three months.

⁓

Have you heard the one about the United States Supreme Court
voting to legislate women's bodies?

What a question!

⁓

The abortion question loves to fool around
masquerading as a lawyer, as an illegally appointed judge.

It plays swashbuckler, predator, and prey.

The question hangs about me like a pest
tugging at my knees. Begs.

It will not go away.

Offers another drink—
a Manhattan, shaken and stirred—

Mother Figure, Almost

I'm thinking about ginger ale—extra dry. The bottle
wrapped in green and gold foil. The first bubbles
humming like a hailstorm of the mind.

Once, my boyfriend's Catholic mother held my arm.
It was high summer.
Your people have such beautiful skin, she cooed brightly

although I knew this was a butchering compliment—
and bewildering since she didn't know my sisters,
had never met my parents. She tasked me as her one,

her only Jew. *Beautiful skin,* the closest she
ever came to showing kindness, stroking my
forearm as the two of us sat hip to hip by the sea.

Two women—extraterrestrials—
from separate solar systems circling each other,
the ragged fault lines between us just facts

like the laws of no lobster, no ham.
That night she orbited my room—twice
to certify—no sexual relations with her son.

Jewish girls are easy, he'd informed me—
My one . . . my only . . . the house rocked
on the edge of a precipice. Downstairs, I heard

glasses clink and crash, as the patriarch sang
broken songs and smashed his fists on the shards—
while his wife sipped gin fizzes in the dark.

The One Good Eye in the Room

When you left, I felt exhausted
and so was the room we fought in.
The front door stammered behind you
and in came silence—a recreational drug,
a fast-forming habit that untied its shoelaces,
sank into the loveseat and prepared to stay
up with me all night.

Survival depends on the breath and its silences—
the in-between spaces and their rumors.
When I claimed silence during our fights, you'd
answer me with anger as if quietness
was a personal affront instead of a house of ruin
where gravity bore down on us—
a horned instrument—all the notes gone.

What if I told you silence worked as a sweetener—
a French eclair or a palm tree vacation where
we could rely on a good time. When you left,
silence looked me in my one good eye, believed in me.
Let's play a game, silence said. *Let's see who
speaks first.* Then we washed and salted
the pasta, the delicately spiced sauce.

My Little Biscuit / My Lemon Peel

All day you bubble into liquid pieces
like a bath's surface, like a showerhead
with its dial of tricks, its pulse.

All day you search for the baobab tree
and mangoes, the dayglow
lizards—the leper ladies

who laugh with you from empty bowls.

Remember Sa-a, his name
which meant *the lucky one*? How hours
hunched like logs no one could move,

time cracking the coffee table, the ledge

of each boys' elbows? You'd hear
the brag of the new Toyota,
your lover shouting *ina kwana,* calling out ~

Remember? The millet fields,
the Nigerian makeup
girls used to bleach their skin,

your neighbor, multilingual and soccer-stricken?

Remember Prince and Freak Out,
the pink of washboard roads,
fast sex without a condom ~

and its predictable results?

Little biscuit, lemon peel,
pig tether—the fetus
that quickly followed, never showed.

Here's the praise song to the almost
child, almost mother, father
~ *almost, almost, almost* ~

And voilá, Habiba, our caretaker

the day you left and didn't know—
the crush of her wise body like a
waterfall, a levy overflowed.

Loss streaming across cow dung and thistle—
And still here, beside the bath, this ghost-child,
dragging waterproof alphabet, soggy cupcake, silent whistle.

Self Portrait with Bee Sting

Last night while watering the garden
I mistakenly elbowed a yellow jacket
or perhaps a carpenter bee

casually bathing in a galaxy

of purple aster. And then, as if
taking the Circle Train home,
we accordioned together vaudeville-style—

our physical margins shaken

by the brokenness of surprise.
Through the torn cloth
of my hip pocket, I feel the stinger

insert until he stumbles, slow motion,

into the flowerpot; inert like a lover
who has overexerted himself,
then lies down in the husk

of a late July night. Now all I have left

of him is a raised scar, burning
like a silver dollar, and swiftly seen-to
with wet tea bags and copper pennies—

the way we try to exorcise toxins

from our lives: a blue basin next to the crib
of a sick infant or a vacuum cleaner
hanging in the guest room closet. When he left

I didn't recognize myself in the drapes.

I took down the mirrors
from the walls, subsisting only on wildflowers
and the machinery of my heartbeat

which came as a continuous surprise—

the new knowledge that
my body could outlast death—
might heal this deep, sharp, sting.

A Second Earth Orbiting a Star

Compass

Elizabeth Bishop often kept a compass
in her small jacket pocket: a little-known fact
about the poet who fell regularly from a delicate
map of sobriety, lost her keys, entire weeks—
even countries. Could a compass—initially used
in fortune-telling, invented in the Han Dynasty—buoy
her with its divining arrow, its quivering and irregular
heartbeat? What are the coordinates of the soul:
mist-filled or incandescent, briny as ocean air or rugged
as Ouro Prêto? Bishop could lose herself in the architecture
of a bird cage, the clack of wooden clogs. But with binoculars
strung around her neck like miniature islands, a compass
in her hand, her brokenness could orient her, her brokenness
could console her like a harbor chart or a naked, pink dog.

Not Monet's Giverny

In our snow globe of goodbyes, we leave
cities burning, arguments still on fire.

We do not touch but force ourselves

into pockets and gloves.
Winter stumbles on: questions

without answers.

Glass bridge of exits, cracked runway lights
flare blue and gold.

We travel through forlorn gates

the size of empty breadbaskets,
do not stop for sweets or tea.

On the last day of this life
we will not live together

we steer north of Paris
to observe the descendants of lily pads,

abandoned in the gardens of Giverny.

Everything frozen.
Even now—decades on,

the same little remains.

Empty beds where the iris had lived,
river stones to an oatmeal sky.

And a man and a woman struck numb.

Burn Barrel

You think I write about you to remember
one sand-lit dinner in the Sahel

but I don't. Not to think of your skin spiced
with cardamom and sweat, nor the bullet

proof smile you kept. Not to hear again
the timbre of your voice—dusk

spangling through my chest like a meteor.
I disliked the mad musician curls

you ignored like your penchant for half-
finished schemes: abandoned and forlorn.

Instead, this is for the final forgetting:
a fire for words like *palaver* and *high-wire*.

Now I live next door to an oolong plantation.
In the center stands a decaying barn

caked in blue manure and honeybees.
I think of you this way—

rotting at the end of the season.
The trouble that's gone and the burn

barrel of delight that went with it.
I write of you to stake a claim

not to make sense of a man who
worshipped only his own words—

who never tried to read the bright leavings
nuanced and telling in mine.

String Theory with Heartache

The long lines of this sentence look to resolve in a point
of punctuation; when in fact, there are still more sentences

      and conditional clauses, and exclamations to go. But what if the point
      is not the point? Under the world's microscope we see that

no picture frame, no old love, no sigh
actually stays still. Maybe we are all made of strings!

      A gull draws a winter branch across the horizon,
      then returns to add a delicate curve to its nest—

Today the news reports a second earth orbiting a neighbor star.
In pampas grass and dried pods of vanilla, in suspension

      bridges and candy floss, what heat works
      to vibrate twigs to filament to universe?

      Perhaps this is why violins
      and guitars, cellos and dulcimers, are so delicious

in our inner ears—a seduction by strings—
building blocks of our own bosons, of cells, of clear waters.

      If we move like jerboas or paddle boarders that circulate
      air over their own limbs,

then we know our disguises are working.
The desert trek on camelback, the Tuareg sash on even longer

          hand-embroidered robes. If we are simply
            balls of twine wound around breaths of air, then how to pluck

and pick our lives—to repair the filament in our ledgers—
the elegant rumors of belief.

Medina, Morning

Past pomegranate sellers, past hand-pulled wagons
stacked skyward with Africa's most delectable bread,

    past riads and *fuduks,* silversmiths and silk weavers;

past courtyard cafes, leather shops, past labyrinth
after labyrinth of glitter and glaze—we negotiate inner passageways

    filled with herbalists, spice merchants, motorcyclists

and a clowder of orange cats—until, suddenly, *L'Art du Bain*
materializes on a spot Google Maps calls: *Unknown.*

    Until the cedar doors open and we enter the sanctuary—

soap mixed from camel milk and night-blooming jasmine, almond blossom
and rose displayed next to jars of black gels and potions, *foutas* and five sugar scrubs—

the scene takes our words away, takes the petrol exhaust from our lungs.

We sample each organic cream, each ointment and oil;
our wrists and arms slick with it, our earlobes and necks, dappled and dabbed.

    And when the beautiful Berber merchant comes back with cups of tea,

he notes our new selves and offers the story of the damask rose from his city
in the High Atlas where petals spangle the streets, where married women rise

    before dawn to gather sand-colored sacks of blossoms which imprint

on their bodies, their bank accounts, their beds. He mimes how the queen floats
at the front of the May parade, the streets transformed into a souk

of coral, and puce; flamingo, magenta, and the shocking pink fingers of dawn.

You are very welcome, he shrugs and slips small gifts into our packs.
His hands scent our own as we leave.

Binocular Vision

What happens to a zygote
who never becomes—
no cartilage to deliver back

to the ground; no evening
meals for the earth-
worm, no morning glory?

Today is your *Happy Non-*
Birthday, 31—perhaps
you would have developed

into a geologist or lounge singer—
keen observer of the disappearing
life. I imagine you the way

politicians often fantasize
about their voters: illogically and
with a little greed.

I had you and then
suddenly, didn't have you.
My insides retracted

by mother, father, sisters:
us two against four.
And I folded to forever

or to that ongoing number,
infinity, where we balance
on bitter ovals of regret.

My spy in the afterlife,
my choiceless choice
like a suicide's

last wish to disappear
by deep water or blood-splashed
bracelets, immolation or

implosion of the heart. Don't
I transform by that same
double-hinge? Half-mother,

half-old crone, longing for
my lovely disembodied—
my dear, body of a boy.

Shadowboxing

That night the air stank, the stars obscured behind wild horses
of clouds. We walked on cobblestones on the edge of something

I could not name: new land of unalterable decisions
like a retinue of assassins coming right for me, who kept coming

in a bad dream that dissolved like a black and white movie, the dark
mouth enveloping the entire screen. *The End.* Then the aftermath

like a heroin addict waking up in the overgrowth of a river path,
no longer young. There are nights that pummel your life, chart

an alternate course unasked for and colorless—the way it was
the first time you encountered the one ready to eat out your heart—

an innocent remark—a joke about ocelots or the weeds of purple carrots.
That night I was caught in a before and after, an unsayable horror film

of half-lives as we hipswayed and grunted along the Seine.
When someone passed us, their teeth shone like those of a vampire

happy with the waste of the world. Ready to drink it in. My body
was four months pregnant, crossing over to a nightmared path

of no return. But isn't this the truth of every moment?
To revise our lives into the *I belong*—to this tribe of the unreliable

narrators, luminous in our stories and in our squalor.

The Decision

Your Still Life Builds a Home Inside My Head

In the late afternoon we lose an f-stop
as light bleeds out of the bandaged sky

and like phantom detectives with wide-brimmed hats

we reexamine the compass, the passport,
the magnetized color of four o'clock air.

In this woman-made harbor, we rearrange

pipe stands and glass slides. We multitask wicker stands
where objects could topple at any time—

let them topple!

Here in the land of deferred decisions,
a hand-painted garden ball reflects on a floating scroll.

In this alchemical mirror, in this ark of a studio—

built on instinct and breath, through windows
clouded and smeared,

under the sign of the light meter

I'll meet you here. A bright space to hold inside my head,
an open country—another life still new.

The Other Side of Paris

If his bathroom hadn't been outside the apartment.
If it hadn't just snowed,
icicles dotting the hallway.

~

Benoit was a believer. Devout.
He shouted; *I am ready to be a father—*
but not a husband.
Weargueandweargueandweare.

~

In our nightmare, I craft a decision—
mail an aerogramme to him.
I'm keeping it, I write though
this might be a kind of lie.

~

Whatever happens to our never-born—
attached to a uterus, washed out in a storm?
toabortionortoabortionor . . .

~

Later, I'll collage together different lives
into a blue shadow box:
unfit mother/absent father/
suicidal offspring—

~

I decide
and undecide
a hundred times an hour.

In Praise of Anger

It has taken so long to find you,
years of squirreling your shadow
back under the bed. And now,

you are here beside me, head
on the pillow, no longer denied.
I spit, sing, state my case—

and the roof does not fly off, the cellar
door remains well hinged. Anger
arcs into prisms, like a starlight

scope on a cool summer night.
Suddenly, I throw the oak tree at it
with ease, flip each ex-lover, the entire

neighborhood—the man next door who shoots
the sunrise, the tree cutter, the cat killer.
I take my anger out of the box and tap it

like a prayer wheel, run its messages along
the rim of the world, without regret—
love it like a child's spinning top.

The Decision

On my hardest day, I dressed, walked
onto the balcony, setting off the system's alarm

in the time when only drug dealers and paranoids

wrapped their houses in Radionics—
the '80s. Days of velour and lycra,

hotpants and Farah Fawcett hairdos.
While I taught high school for Peace Corps in West Africa,

banks installed computers that dispensed dollar bills

asking each of us to type in a secret password.
I wanted a word that would open up my life.

Grocery stores began using barcodes—

how did the silent square know so much?
The Walkman appeared, and the mixtape rose in stature.

I was a mixtape—baby or no baby?

What was the code to bring my delinquent fiancé home?
And the damn bells kept ringing—

I'm keep it, was all I wrote on the postcard,

except this was in French. I'm keeping myself
was what it said. And I posted the fragmented

blues and fiery reds to his last known Paris address.

I'm keeping it, I said as I left the wailing in my brain,
the alarm now inside and outside the apartment—

then the body no longer my body but a cathedral

of past seductions seemed to disappear; and so, I did
what was asked for: I headed towards the abortion

dr. and strolled off the balcony into the land of the dead.

Weeping Glass

Here a 17th century wineglass
displays early signs of instability—
a spot of silver smoke

lingers along the opening of the mouth—
one rogue layer of iridescence.

Imagine now the world's unseen glass objects,
forgotten in museum basements—
vessels, mosaics, flowers—

with ghost traces of fine lines.

Include picture frames leaning in catalogued stacks—
so many oils and watercolors, early photographs,
lithographs, pastels.

Weeping Glass, the curator calls it,
caused by chemical imbalances.

An affected edge begins to cloud,
then bead, then tiny, silvered lines:
runes we no longer know how to read.

The art piece starts to fracture
each community declaring its losses.

Like the nearly lost fragments of a life
which insist upon themselves
each morning before sunrise—

history staging its own protest.

Like citizens, who in the thousands
crossed the Brooklyn Bridge just yesterday
for Amadou Diallo, Brianna Taylor, George Floyd—

like spectral voices and cut glass—

like our unclaimed memory through shards of decency
as we transform the cracks to light.

A Blessing for Absence

To hear the luxury of heat
pulse through air ducts—

its whistles and bumps,
to readjust the bedcovers

against uninfected skin
and move the sliding window

wide open—to listen
to the dogs' dark chorus

in the well of night—
absence of ambulance, of helicopter—

to declare, *I am*, holding
on as the plum branches

beat against the roof,
as rainwater bellows

through damaged drainpipes.
How did I arrive here—

with a passion for this September's
catalogue of tools, an art-deco

umbrella stand, a slide rule.
To the pleasure of what is absent—

no unmarked graves, no imminent
evictions. Then what is this heaviness

embedded in our good luck—
this sharp, bronzed hinge?

Single, Taken, Not Interested ✓

This year I have ascended to rock star status,
inductee in the Hall of Fame.

I've achieved Olympic Gold for sleeping

solo in a single bed, a bank of pillows
saved just for me. At dawn, I grind

my coffee beans just so, no one's honking snores

bother me. Pecan toast and a bowl of *Cheerios,*
a torn T-shirt and wrinkle cream.

This is how it is done. Every day deranged

into a holiday. The judge banished from his chambers—
the accountant no longer itemizing my indiscretions—

I caress madrona trees & binge on an Italian

detective series. Unbridled laughter. I buy twice baked
biscuits, dip them in marmalade with clotted cream.

The clocks click along contentedly, each one set

for a different time. I've watercolors to create,
a shoreline to walk, a trip around the world to take—

on my own. My friend divorced after forty years, confides

that while in her marriage she could not
name her favorite color or which song she preferred to sing.

Another friend confesses she never embraced

even one *night stuck on my own.* I appoint myself
the high priestess of the newly single—write sermons

on how to stretch ecstatically into the first person singular—

the proud "I" that does not apologize,
the "I" that no one holds by the throat.

Safed Palmist

According to the Kabala, the way palmistry works is that when a soul is garbed in a body, it becomes imprinted there, particularly on the hands.

I bought a rabbi one hot afternoon.
His floor replete with Bar Mitzvah boys asleep;

a library of boys in wrinkled shirts,
their rinds of oranges strewn like spiral ghosts.

Then he took my hand, startled by what he saw.
In Hebrew lines that sprung like pomegranate seeds—

my life in proverbs, old language, unadorned:
please, do not leave yourself again.

The temperature created mirages in the air
which shimmered like water, like waves, like tears,

as my translator looked on, then looked away.
I watched a younger self dissolve; forgave

her lies, her dalliances, her earthbound skirt
of need as his wife sang half notes undisturbed,

a violet flavored lozenge on the porch.
Then he found my heart line, touched the break—

Safed, Israel

Star Map

Dear H,

How strange to think of you this way—
H as dangerous.
H as demented.

I was schooled to crave you
like powdered sugar,

or *Roman Holiday,*
elegant suites with ocean views.

The symptoms of my diagnosis?

Bright fever of adoration
for another life—
one with more dollars in my pockets.

O Happiness, how well you ignore the struggle.

Our city is full of false faces,
Italian suits almost no one can afford to buy.

One day we're best friends
and the next you've tossed out my number.

You're a mescal so addictive,
all the girls want you—
dazzled by the bright worm of promise.

What a flâneur
you turned out to be—
a harlot, a sphinx, a haint of a god.

Curriculum Vitae

after L.M.

1. In the year of my birth, *Anne Frank* appeared as a Broadway play. Mother ate caraway seeds. Bit down hard.

2. I was brought into a family of changelings.

3. At the bottom of the stairs, father called out, "It's the Boston Strangler," a joke that delighted me, his youngest daughter.

4. (There were maps of Lithuania and Russia where grandparents ran from, dragging pillowcases of hazelnuts and silver. Never mentioned again.)

5. After school, I searched mother's dresser drawers for clues of our identity: ripped photographs, repaired nylons, Miss Liberty dimes, and a girdle.

6. In the old language, the parents exchanged nests of secrets: *putz, alta cocker, tuchas leker.*

7. The potato kugel and gefilte fish, strudel and krepla: bright lintels into the past. Repeating each consonant calibrated its own entryway back in time.

8. The family's toehold into the middle class sent the teenager fleeing into the past. She wanted parallel lives, the alchemy of windows which open into the past. Also, the Saharan desert; Sarajevo, Marrakesh. An infinity of fresh starts.

9. The imaginary lover seems a little late. Running behind schedule.

10. Sometimes the single life feels like a painting in plein air; sometimes an ice cave.

11. I watched mother ready herself for death.

12. Stoic, except for brief tears.
    A life of trying hard not to feel
    finally left her unable to speak.

13. And then suddenly, three decades in the Northwest.
    Flickers and stellar jays. Sonnets.

14. No nuclear life. No child calling out—

15. Father taught me to scramble an egg, perfect a waffle;
    to love angel wing begonias and discern the specific
    knock of a cantaloupe, to test for sweetness.

16. One day, men no longer looked at me. I remember there was a storm
    and then a sunrise obscured in clouds.

17. The hours twinkle and irridesse. Sometimes after midnight, I steady myself
    conversing with stars, readying for the world-to-come in a constellation of longing.

18. ... --- / ..-. .- .-. / ... --- / --. --- --- -.. / ... --- / ..-. .- .-. / ... --- / --. --- --- -..

Abeyance

Today my friend told me of her girl's hand-dug coffin;
how in Antarctica, training to stay alive meant to pickaxe,

crack, and cut, until a furrow the size of a brown bear
appears and her graduate school daughter descends

into a trench barely length-wise enough for her
sleeping sac; eventually sealed-off with a brick of snow.

An ice coffin, the mother told me, gently recalling how
her offspring slipped beneath the crust of the world.

How the hours spent warming hands in armpits was worth it.
To survive the woman relied on her own muscle work—

a lacey box of molecules and the animal beat of her heart.
At dusk with the exercise completed, the men disappeared

to hot showers, a dinner of ribs in the ranger station,
but her daughter remained underground. She had labored

for hours and was determined to sleep beneath the ice.
And then suddenly, the next morning as she climbed up—solidly

alive, stunned by the machinery of her own body.
I like to believe she knew herself as different—

changed as Persephone had changed, into a new woman—
lifted into a blue abeyance—beyond the self and climbing.

Dear Benoit,

Remember when we did it in the middle of a millet field
under an audience of equatorial stars?
I remember the hungry stalks, no rain for months
swallowed whole our arguments, our hard knuckled
yeses and nos. Together we completed an androgynous body,
beyond mortal, forever conjoined by this bomber moon,
earth-lit in blue projections.

And afterward, united by the high
window as your hips pressed against my undress—
I knew we had made love to the universe.
The solar systems all-in on our game of rise-up and fall;
the after-midnight moment, the mad promise of the gods—
an ascension into the world where we emerged
utterly triumphant, for one moment, entirely forged.

Republic of Niger, West Africa

Crepe Myrtle

I should have been a crepe myrtle, resistant to pests and disease—
should have been known by my nicknames: *Purple Magic, Ebony Flame.*

I'd have passed my life as a hip resting spot for cardinals, larks, and bluetits.
Could have been a pine siskin—an elegant flash of wing. Been a star

magnolia, close to extinction in the wild, child world—
sexy as a fragrant fringe cup drinking it up along riverbeds. A salmon-

berry. A lady fern. I should have kept the baby. All the best flowers,
single blooms. All the boy birds, yellow-bellied sap suckers.

Could have nested in the cavity of a blue atlas; become a field
note, bilingual, old; fought romantic battles with stinging nettles—

avoided mildew and armored scale. Now I night jasmine,
I honeysuckle, I myrtle—requiring little water or microbial soil.

Schmitz Preserve, West Seattle, WA

From the Dictionary of Obscure Sorrows

Last spring, I walked with you to the lilac trees.
We took home contraband branches of shadow

and scent as if we were the finest magicians
conjuring perfumes from tiny blossoms

that the Victorian women planted
to mark the loss of a child or a miscarriage.

I choose not to love you and so the globes
remained just broken remnants of minerals,

skeletons left over from the latest skirmish.
Please don't ask me to explain the Dictionary

of Obscure Sorrows. I couldn't if I wanted to
but I know there's an entry here for me—

something about the long hallways of
dormitories once the students depart

or the afterhours drinking in amusement parks
where you catch the shellacked eye

of the carousel horse and nod *hello*.
I've always desired a different life than the one I am living.

It's an invisible cloak I wear like a fog-lit figure
in a Bergman film or maybe I'm more like the goat's

cello in the off-center village of a Chagall painting
that tells me with blue certainty, *you're not alone*.

Still Life with Ladder

Today, the sky saved my life
caught between smoked rum and cornflower.
Today, there is a color I can't name cruising past

the back door—it is the idea of color.
Cloudscapes evaporate like love songs
across lost islands, each a small bit coin of thought.

Today, I am alive and this is a good thing—

clams in the half shell, a lemon rosemary tart.
I live in the day and the day lives past me.
If I could draw a map of the hours, a long

horizon would travel on indefinitely ~ a green, backlit thread.

The sky? It is never the same—it is sour milk
and whipped cream, a sketchbook and flour-dusted jeans.
Today, I am in love with the sky.

It doesn't care if my father is dead,
or that I live by myself with his Masonic watch.
I sew time with my mother's button jar.

I've improvised my life—let the sky pull the strings.

Tonight, I will borrow the golden ladder from the orchard,
travel from this sphere into the next and expunge
the leftover sadness of the hemispheres, to move beyond

the beyond which is here, present, alive in this hyacinth room;

time leaps over itself, after and out of the tangled past
overshadows weather falling across a back window—
to forgive one another; to try once more to live it right.

Hello, July 5th!

The morning is full of embarrassed flowers
lost in maritime light—
friends to the man on my street
who sweeps the sidewalk with an imaginary broom.
I hear the howl of the huskies next door,
the gunfire of the beachcombers, the madness
of the kitchen clock calculating the minutes
for a sockeye salmon or the secondhand arm
working itself up to the unknown half-second
of my death. *Thanks, kitchen clock!*

By the fireplace and under the stairs,
there's shingles to look forward to
and the demise of supporting beams—
decades of repair and replace.
How does it feel to play cancer roulette
on the accordion of time?
Better to burn up the past, except
for aunt molly as she cursed
perfection—the search for the favorite shade
of the favorite color, or man, or love seat.

Hello July 5th! Let's sing down 60th Avenue.
Hipsway to sexy tunes only we can hear.
Hello summer of 2021! Hello! Hello! There's cash enough
for organic salads and orgasms with the organ grinder's
left-hand man. And why not?
It's not madness to make such proclamations.
or, for that matter, to waltz with a potted plant.
No need to be embarrassed.
The fog lifts her layered skirts,
slowly making her way from the tidal demands of the sea.

How else to live except by reanimating joy
the way the wind sways the plumtree's branches,
the way the sugar ants barge in, wanted or not.
The way the shingle outside my house swings.
Hello, Lovelies—the optimist agent is in.

Attempting Speculative Fiction

There's a space inside me like a tree house

topped with wisteria vine, the windows
point like a compass to my second self,

where S strides in past globes and oceans,

walks up to the bar says, *whisky neat,*
without the please.

Says nothing about sorrow.

I listen from somewhere faraway
as she holds the floor with her bookish looks,

the season's *don't fuck with me* boots.

She's an actor or a double agent—
all five-card stud, chiseled cheekbones, and hopes.

Yet, here in my house with triple-locks

and wireless alarms, my mortgaged heart—
I wonder how she will get home—

what catastrophe might follow.

I write down the thousand different things
the world might do and then erase them

to the young girl who walked out, who didn't lock the door.

NOTES

"Metaphors" takes its inspiration from Sylvia Plath's poem "Metaphors," which focuses on the nature of pregnancy.

The form of "Post-Abortion Questionnaire—Powered by Survey Monkey" takes its inspiration (with thanks) from Oliver de la Paz's "Autism Questionnaire."

"The Abortion Question" references the murders of women while they sat in two preterm healthcare clinics in Brookline, Massachusetts. *Clinic shooting suspect John Salvi captured: N.H. man held in Brookline deaths after Virginia facility hit.* Boston Globe, January 1, 1995. The form is inspired by Patricia Lockwood's "The Rape Joke."

"Your Still Life Builds a Home Inside My Head" is dedicated to the American-Canadian performance artist, photographer, jazz singer, and surrealist Carol Sawyer.

"Blue Dusk" borrows its title from poet, mentor, and former nun Madeline DeFrees (1919–2015).

"Abeyance" is for Lisa C. Taylor.

"High Atlas Incantation" and "Medina, Morning" locate themselves in Central Morocco and are dedicated to filmmaker, poet, translator, traveler, and dearest friend Angie Vorhies.

Biographical Note

Susan Rich is the author of eight books, including *Gallery of Postcards and Maps: New and Selected Poems*, as well as *Cloud Pharmacy, The Alchemist's Kitchen, Cures Include Travel*, and *The Cartographer's Tongue: Poems of the World*. Her poetry has earned her awards from the Fulbright Foundation, PEN USA, and the *Times Literary Supplement* (London). Individual poems appear in the *Harvard Review, New England Review, O Magazine*, and *Poetry Ireland*, among other places. Susan is coeditor with Kelli Russell Agodon of *Demystifying the Manuscript: Creating a Book of Poems*. She teaches at Highline College and directs Poets on the Coast: A Writing Retreat for Women from Seattle, Washington.

Printed in the USA
CPSIA information can be obtained
at www.ICGtesting.com
JSHW021401250324
59871JS00005B/151